Syrian Christian Names

– *Their Meaning and Origin*

By Kurien Verghese

Table of Contents

Foreword

Why do we require a name? A name is a term used for identification. We want to distinguish one object from another. Persons acquire names, to enable the public or the community to identify them or distinguish them from others.

The Bible gives a lot of importance to Names. In the New Testament, the angel of the Lord told Zachariah to name his son John (who later was known as John the Baptist). The same angel went to Joseph and told him to name his son Jesus (meaning deliverer from sins). The Lord's Prayer starts with 'Our Father in Heaven, hallowed be Thy Name', which is a way to say, 'May God's name be Holy'. It goes back to the Jewish tradition and their customs around names. The Jews named their children to identify them physically and to reflect their nature. In the Old Testament, God has many names in Hebrew, to reflect His many characteristics.

 In India, for the Hindus, naming a child is sacred and they have a special naming ceremony generally called 'Namkaran'.
The Christians have a Baptism or Christening ceremony where the new born child is given a formal Christian name. The Syrian Christians follow this tradition.

The following chapters are my research on the meaning, origin and history of **Syrian Christian Names.**

Syrian Christian Names

Brief History of the Community

The Syrian Christians are a Christian community, originally from Kerala, in the south west corner of India. The general opinion is that they are called 'Syrian Christians', because they conduct their church worship using Syriac liturgy.

The Syrian Christians of Kerala lived for a thousand and more years in Kerala side by side with the Hindus, absorbed some customs and manners from the Hindu Nair Community, but still closely retained their identity and Christian traditions. It is said that "Syrian Christians are Indian in culture, Christian in faith and Syrian in liturgy".

According to the traditions of the Syrian Christians of Kerala, St. Thomas, one of the apostles of Jesus Christ landed at Kodungallore (Cranganoor), north of the present-day Kochi, in AD52. There he converted some local Namboothiri (Malayalee Hindu Brahmin) families to Christianity and the present day Syrian Christians are mainly the progeny of such Namboothiri converted Christians. About AD 345, immigrants from Chaldea and places near present West Asia, under the leadership of Knai Thomman landed in Kerala, probably trying to escape persecution in their motherland. The descendants of these immigrant Christians and those of the Namboothiri Christians, together became the Nazranis or Syrian Christians of Kerala. The name Nazrani was a reference to being followers of Jesus of Nazareth.

Note: The story of St Thomas converting Namboothiris has been strongly challenged by several historical researchers. According to them, Namboothiri's came to Kerala around the 3rd century (from a little further north or west of India).

Syrian Christian Names

Today, there are two main divisions among the Syrian Christians; the majority belong to the Roman Catholic Church and acknowledge the supremacy of the Pope. The others are Orthodox and off shoots of Orthodox Christians.

In addition, there is a group that is a part of Church of South India, which generally follows the practices of the Church of England. There are also groups belonging to the newer churches or denominations like the Pentecostal, Brethren, Methodists etc. but most of them or their ancestors belonged to the Orthodox churches and come under the general term Syrian Christians. Note, Latin Christians and Nadar Christians are not Syrian Christians.

Syrian Christian Name Origins

Biblical Origins

The names of the Syrian Christians are from the Bible, but a good number of the names have been Malayalamized (that is localized in Malayalam, the language of Kerala).

To find the original Biblical names, one should go to the Syriac or Greek Bible; as they may not appear accurately in the English Bible.

The names given in the Malayalam Bible are almost the same as in the Syriac/Greek version. Jesus Christ spoke Aramaic (Syria was called Aram) and Aramaic was spoken in parts of Palestine or what is now known as West Asia. This Aramaic language later gave birth to the Syriac language. The Bible was translated into Malayalam from Syriac in the 1800's by Christian priests from Syria, who were missionaries to Kerala.

One must be extremely circumspect when dealing with the English versions of names of persons or places because the English distorted the original names of persons and places which came under their imperial rule. For example, the original name of Jesus was Yeshu, changed to Jesus by the English. His mother was Mariam or Myriam, not Mary.

Syrian Christian Names

Naming Traditions

The original mother tongue of Nazranis was not Malayalam. It was a Dravidian/Tamilian dialect in the 1st Century. Malayalam became a distinct and a separate language only by 10th century AD. The early Nazranis had many Dravidian or Tamil names and some of these names were retained, and are still in use.

Syrian Christians have a tradition of naming their first son after the child's father's father (paternal grandfather). The second son is named after his mother's father. Similarly, the first daughter takes the name of her paternal grandmother (father's mother), the second daughter takes the name of her maternal grandmother. Usually the third, fourth children are given their paternal and maternal uncle even grand uncles names or the names of their aunts/grand aunts.

Catholic Names

 Some names commonly prevalent among the Catholic Christians of Kerala have been omitted, as they are the names of Saints of Latin or European origin. This usage of western names started only after the arrival of the Portuguese in Kerala (in the 1500's) and are not of Nazrani origin. These are names like Antony, Sebastian etc.

Syrian Christian Names

Interpretation Guidelines

Given below are some of the rules or guidelines followed in interpreting Syrian Christian names.

1. The Old Testament books were written mostly in Hebrew and the New Testament books were written in Greek. Therefore, one should consider the Hebrew and Greek versions respectively to find the correct names and their meanings, not the English Bible. I am relying on the Malayalam Bible for the correct names, including the pronunciation, as it followed the Syriac version, which followed the Hebrew/Greek version.

2. The Greek names end in 'os' or 'ose' while the Latin version ends in 'us'. The new Testament books were written in Greek. The Gospel writers Mark and Luke were Markose, Lukose in Greek, and Marcus, Lucus in Latin. By dropping these suffixes, we get the English equivalent.

3. Many of the Nazrani names follow the Malayalam practices, of the male names ending in 'an' or 'en'. Names like Thoma changed to Thommen in Malayalam.

4. Names have been colloquialized. Malayalam is a Dravidian language very much akin to Tamil. The early Syrian Christians spoke Tamil or a dialect of Tamil before Malayalam was a language.
    There used to be no 'ba' sound in Tamil and the Dravidians found it difficult to pronounce the 'ba' or 'be' sound. The word 'Abba' meaning father is the same as 'Appa' meaning father in Tamil and Malayalam.

Similarly, the sound 'Ga' was almost never used till the Sanskritisation of Malayalam started, it was substituted by the 'Ka' sound. (Varghese and Varky).

5. When two vowels are joined, in Malayalam it is connected by a "v' or 'va' sound but in Tamil by a 'y'or 'i' sound. For example, the southern town of Nagerkoil in Kanya-Kumari district, in Tamil Nadu was Nagerkovil, when it was a part of Travancore. The ko-v-il of Malayalam reverted to ko-y-il of Tamil. Similarly, Thiru-ananthapuram becomes Thiruvananathapuram, in Malayalam, with a 'v' between Thiru and Ananthapuram.

6. When a name is written in English, people use different spellings to write the same name. For example: the name 'Varghese' can be written Verghese, Varughese, Varghis, Verghis, Warghese, but it is one and the same in Malayalam and should be treated as one name.

7. Many names among the Syrian Christians have prefixes and suffixes which are not integral to the names, and therefore should not be treated as a separate name. Here are a few examples:
   a. Kunju and Kutty - meaning baby/small/junior in Malayalam. Kunju is the prefix to many names like Kunju Thoma. Kutty is a commonly used suffix like Thomas Kutty. Both should be treated the same as Thoma or Thomas for the purposes of knowing its origin/meaning.
   The Kutty suffix is also used by Hindus and Muslims of Kerala. Example Raman Kutty, Krishnan Kutty, among Hindus; Ibrahim Kutty, among Muslims. Women also have 'Kutty' attached to their names; example Maria Kutty, Madhavi Kutty.

b. Men have 'achan' attached as a suffix. Achan means father, and is used as a term of respect or endearment. Ex Chackochan i.e. Chacko Achan, Thomachan i.e. Thoma Achan. They are treated as Chacko and Thoma.

c. Women have 'Amma' as a suffix. Amma means mother, the suffix amma is used as a mark of respect. Syrian Christian names such as Mariamma, and Saramma should be treated as Maria and Sarah.

8. When English education started in Kerala, people started using the corresponding English names of their Syrian or Nazrani names. Thus, names like John, Joseph, George became very commonly used by the Nazranis instead of Yohannan or Ouseph. Such names as John, Joseph, George are not Syrian Christian or Nazrani names in origin; they are names widely used by the contemporary Syrian Christians because of their English origin.

9. A note about Indian Names: The names of people in many communities in India can be distinguished by their endings. In India, Rama, Krishna are all names of Gods. In Tamil and Malayalam, masculine names end in 'an' or 'en'. It is Raman, Krishnan, Gopalan, n in Tamil and Malayalam. It is Rama, Krishna, Gopala in Kannada. In North India, it is further shortened to Ram, Gopal, Govind. Syrian Christian names also end in 'an' or 'en', like Thoma to Thommen.

Syrian Christian Male Names

* Denotes that the name is not Nazrani, but widely used by them (from English origin)

NAME	MEANING AND ORIGIN
1. Abraham	**Meaning**: Father of Nations. **Origin**: Derived from the Old Testament. 'Ab' stands for Abba or father. Abu, Abo all denote Father. The Hebrew name was Abram but God changed his name in Genesis to Abraham. Among Syrian Christians Avraham, Avira all are variants of Abraham with 'Ab' pronounced as in abnormal.
2. Alexander* Alexandreose	**Meaning**: Defender of Men. Alex means defender and Andreose means man, Alexandreose in Greek means defender of men. **Origin**: In Greek Mythology, Alexandros was another name of the Trojan Prince Paris, who kidnapped Helen of Troy and started the Trojan war. Omit the Greek suffix 'ose' and we get Alexandre or Alexander as the English name. Alexandreose being a long name, the Malayalees have shortened it to 'Idi Chandy' or just Chandy. Please refer to Chandy.

3. Anthrayose/ Andreos	**Meaning**: Man, Manly. **Origin**: New Testament, Jesus's first disciple, Andrew is the brother of Peter. Andreos in Greek is Andrew in English. The Syrian Christian name retains the 'ose' and is pronounced as 'Anthrayose.'
4. Benjamin*/ Benyamin	**Meaning**: Ben means 'son' and Benyamin is 'son of my right hand' or 'beloved son'. **Origin**: Old Testament, Hebrew Name. Benjamin was the 12th son of Jacob and Rachel. The 'Y" in Hebrew names is changed to "J" when translated in to English. Even in Arabic. Ben means 'son of'. For example: Ben Hur, Ben Bella etc.
5. Behanan	This is NOT a commonly used name. There are some who believe that it is derived from Benjamin. But many who have Behanans in their families claim that it is another form of Yohanan. (Ninan is also a variation of Yohanan).
6. Chacko	**Meaning**: Grabber. **Origin**: Yakob (in Malayalam OT), or Yakub, (derived from Arabic). The 'Y' in Hebrew becomes 'J' in English. The English name is Jacob. Refer to Jacob for meaning.

7. Chandy	**Meaning:** Defender of Men. See Alexander. **Origin**: It is the abbreviated form of Idi-Chandy which in Greek is Alexandreose and Alexander in English. The short/diminutive name of Alexander is Sandy in English. The 'Xander/Sander' is shortened to Sandy. In Malayalam, 'ose' of Alexandreose is omitted to become (Alek-sander) and then to Idik-Sandy and further to Idichandy and then shortened to Chandy. In short, the Malayalam Chandy is the same the English Sandy.
8. Cherian	**Meaning**: Remembrance of God. Please see Zachariah. **Origin**: Old Testament Hebrew name from Zacheria or Zachariah. The Malayalees shortened Zacheria to Cheria. This name Cheria is used by the Syrian Christians but as stated earlier, the masculine names usually end up with an 'an' or an 'en'. So Cheria became Cherian.
9. Chummar	This is the Nazrani equivalent of Simon or Simeon. See Simon below.

<u>Syrian Christian Names</u>

10. Cyriac	**Meaning:** Lord or Lordly **Origin:** Greek. Refer to Kuriakose. Kuriak comes from Kuriak-ose with the suffix 'ose' removed. In Greek, the letter 'y' is the equivalent of English 'u' or short 'oo'. Kuriak in English was originally Kyriak in Greek. In English 'c' often replaces 'k'. (In words like cat, car, cut the letter 'c' is used to represent the 'k' sound). Just like Kaiser became Caesar in English, Kyriak became Cyriac.
11. Cyril	**Meaning**: Lordly. **Origin**: Originated from the Greek name Kyrilose or Cyrilose. Drop the 'ose' and the English form becomes Cyril. See Kurilose. Note: Saint Cyril was a 9th Century Greek missionary to the Slavs and created the Cyrillic alphabet to translate the Bible to Slavic.
12. Daniel	**Meaning**: God is my Judge. **Origin:** Derived from Old Testament. 'El' at the end of a name refers to Elohi or God. There are many Jewish names that end in 'el' like Bethuel, Gamaliel, Nathaniel, Samuel. El is like 'esh' in Indian names – the 'esh' stands for Eshwar or God. Examples are Ramesh, Rajesh, Suresh, Ganesh.

13. David/ Daveed	**Meaning**: Beloved. It was the name of the greatest king of the Jews, King David. **Origin**: Taken from English. In the Malayalam Bible it is David but the pronunciation of 'Da' is as in 'Darwin' and is pronounced as Daveed. The Syrian Christian variants of this name are Tharu (from 'Dawood'), Tharian (Tharu ending with an 'an' for male names in Malayalam).
14. Devassy	This name is mainly used by the Catholic Syrian Christians in Kerala. By using pronunciation (and spelling also) it may appear to be derived from David, Davis, Devassy. The general opinion among Syrian Catholics is that Devassy is Sebastianos.
15. Easo/ Eashow	This is the same as Yeshua meaning Savior. (Please note the similarity between Eashow and Eshwar).

16. Eapen / Epen	**Meaning**: See Stephen and Job. **Origin**: There are two opinions on the origin of this name. 1. The name originates from Job. In the Malayalam Bible, Job is referred to as Iyyob or Eyyob. Eyyob changed to Eyyoben in some areas, and when 'b' became 'p' in Malayalam, then Eyyoben became 'Eyyopen' and that after some usage became E-appan or Eapen (In Thrissur- Kunnamkulam areas, Eapen is pronounced as E-appen). 2. The other opinion is that Epen is Stephen. When 'St' is dropped it becomes Epen. Apart from that, 'Stephen' is Esteben in Spanish and Malayalam. When 'b' was changed to 'p' by the Dravidians, then Esteben became Estepen. Est-Epen was then shortened to Epen. I am of the opinion that both could be correct. When long names are shortened, sometimes, two different names get the same short form. For example, Herbert, Robert and Bertram all get the short nick name of 'Bert'. Similarly, both Job and Stephen could end up as Epen but Stephen is the preferable explanation. There is a Jewish name, Eben, currently in use but does not appear to be Biblical and therefore not the origin of Epen.

17. Eipe/ Iype/Ipe	**Meaning**: Persecuted. See Job. **Origin**: Old Testament Job. In the Malayalam Bible, Job is referred to as Eyyob or Iyyob or Iyyub. In Arabic, Syriac, Hebrew and allied languages, 'a','e' and 'i' sounds are very often interchangeable. Abraham of Hebrew became Ibrahim in Arabic. The very common 'Al' in Arabic becomes 'El' in Hebrew.' The corresponding name for Eyyob/ Iyyub is Ayyub in Arabic. In early Malayalam, the 'b' sound became the 'p' sound, so, Ayyub was pronounced as Ayyup or Ayup. Going backwards: Eipe-Aipe-Ayup-Ayub-Iyyob i.e. Job in English. Another way to understand this, is to look at the Malayalam word 'Sayip' or 'Saippu', which means white man. 'Saip' is derived from the Hindi word 'Sahib" (a respected person). All White men were referred to as Sahibs during their reign in India. The letter 'h' is very often silent and is omitted especially in names (ex. Hanna becomes Anna). So, Sahib became Saib and in Dravidian languages, 'b' is pronounced like 'p', Sahib became 'Saip' or 'Saippu'. This reasoning can explain 'Ayub' to 'Ayup' to Eipe. Note: Mr. S.G Pothen in his book on Syrian Christians says that Eipe is the same as Ouseph which is Joseph in English. Mr. Pothen has not given any supporting reasons and I do not support this view.

18. George*/ Gee Varghese	**Meaning**: Geo means the 'earth'. George or Geevarghese meant one who sustains from the earth, a farmer. **Origin**: George does not appear in the Bible. It is very common among Syrian Christians. This name is the English version of the Malayalam name Gee Varghese. The original Greek name appears to be George-ose or Giorgiose. (Both 'G's are pronounced as God or get). When the 'ose' is dropped, the name became popular as George. Saint George or Georgeose Sahada (Saint in Aramaic) or 'punyavalan' (Saint/Martyr in Malayalam) was a popular saint belonging to the area of ancient Syria. When the Christians of that area migrated to Kerala, St. George remained a popular saint and many were named Georgeose after the Saint. George and Verghese are from the same name Georgeose or Gee Orgheose. See Verghese below.
19. Idichandy/ IdikChandy	Please refer to Chandy. **Origin**: Greek from Alexandreose. Drop the Greek suffix 'ose' to get Alek -Sandre. Sandre became Sandy and then Chandy and Alek was Malayalamised into Idik.

20. Idiculla/ Idikullah	**Meaning**: Defender of /from God **Origin**: The origin and meaning are a bit difficult to divine but many are of the opinion that since Idichandy means Alexander, Idikullah is also Alexander or it could be a similar name. Ul-lah (from Idik-ul-lah) means 'of'' Lah (Al Lah is God). We have seen that Alexander is a double word, Aleks and Ander meaning defender and man respectively. Idik is the same as Aleks meaning defender. Therefore Idik-ullah means Defender of God. It must be remembered that Syrian Christian have another name like this: Math-ul lah (Please see Mathulla and Mathew). The Orthodox Christians had bishops/patriarchs named Abd-ul-lah, Ahat-ul-lah etc.
21. Inasu or Eenasu	**Meaning**-Fiery. **Origin**: In Greek, it is Ignatiose. The English equivalent is Ignatius. Ignatious is used mainly by the Catholics in Kerala. The name Inasu is generally confined to Trissur/Kunnamkulam area.

22. Isaac*/ Issahak	**Meaning**: "he laughs", reflecting Sarah's response when told that she would have a child. **Origin**: The Biblical name is Issahaq, son of the Old Testament patriarch Abraham. In Malayalam also, it is Issahak and colloqually 'Itthak'. The English name is Isaac and the Syrian Christians generally prefer Isaac to Issahak. Isaac married Rebecca and their son Jacob was also called Israel.
23. Ittoop	Refer to Joseph.
24. Itthappiri	This has two origins. This name is mainly confined to Kunnamkulam area of Kerala. To many, Itthapiri is the Kunnamkulam version of Isaac. Isaac is Ithak in Malayalam and Ithapiri is derived from Ithak. This view is subscribed to by some Ithapiris. Another view, is that it is a counter part of Stephanos. The corresponding Malayalam name is Isthephan. This Isthephan morphed to Isthephiri and Ithapiri. As stated earlier, one name could be traced to two different names as was Epen to Iyyob (Job) or Stephen.

25. Itty	**Meaning**: In Malayalam, there is a word 'Ittu' meaning 'a bit' or 'a little'. So 'Itty' maybe the same as ''Kutty' or small. **Origin**: Some Ittys are officially known as Abraham, while they are just Itty or Itty-achan or Ittykunju to the members of their family and friends. A careful study would show that most or all these Ittys are Ittyerahs or Itty-Avirah. Since Avirah is Abraham, they presumed Itty also to be Abraham. This presumption is clearly mistaken, as there are Itty Cherias and Itty Eipes, who might be known as Ittys but are not Abraham. The Hindus also use the name 'Itty' for men and women. In conclusion, Itty is a prefix which later came to be used as a name by itself.
26. Jacob*/ Yacob	**Meaning**: Grabber. **Origin**: Old Testament. Yacob in Greek, and Ya'agov in Hebrew or Yakub from Arabic. The Malayalam Bible name is Yakob/Yacob. English equivalent is Jacob. Jacob is the son of Isaac and Rebecca in the Old Testament. He was 'grabbing' his twin brother Easu's heel when he was born. Syrian Christians use Jacob more frequently than Yacob. The most commonly used name for Jacob is Chacko. See Chacko.

Syrian Christian Names

27. James*	**Meaning:** James means the same as Jacob-Grabber. **Origin**: The Old Testament uses the name Yacob in Greek and Ya'aqov in Hebrew. The same name is translated as James in the English New Testament. The Malayalam Bible translates the Patriarch Jacob's name as Yakob and also the name of disciple James as Yakob. The English name James is used by the Syrian Christians commonly like George or John.
28. Job*	**Meaning**: Persecuted. **Origin**: Old Testament. Job is a righteous man and central character in the Book of Job, who is tested by God. Hebrew name is Iyyov, Arabic name is Ayyub. Job is used by the Nazranis mainly in the Thrissur/Kunnamkulam area. Please see Eipe, the Malayalam name for Job.
29. John*/ Yohannan	**Meaning**: Yahweh/God is Gracious. **Origin**: The original Hebrew name is 'Yehohanan' meaning Yehova is gracious. Yehohanan was shortened to Yohannan in Hebrew. It is also Yohannan in Malayalam. Other forms of Yohannan are Ulahannan, Behanan, Ninan and Lonan. The short name is Yohan. The English name is John. Other forms of John are Johann, Juan, Ivan and Giovanni. John is one of the twelve disciples of Christ and author of John 1, 2 and 3 and Revelations.

30. Joseph*	**Meaning**: He will add. **Origin**: Old Testament, Hebrew name is Yosef. He was the 11th son of Jacob and the first son with Jacob's wife Rachel. The English form is Joseph. Other forms are Yoseph, Yusef, Ouseph, Uthup and it further morphed to Ittoop especially in Thrissur/ Kunnamkulam area.
31. Joshua*	**Meaning**: Yahweh (God) is Salvation. **Origin**: Old Testament name of the companion to Moses was Joshua. The Hebrew name is Yehoshua. The Aramaic short form is written as Yeshu'a or Yeshu for short. Please see Koshy below.
32. Koshy	**Meaning**: God is Salvation. See Joshua. **Origin**: In Greek, Joshua is written as Ghosuae. 'J' and 'G' are similar sounding and in many cases interchangeable. In many European languages, the name 'George' is written as 'Jorge'. So 'Ghosuae' became Joshua in English. Since 'gh' sounds like 'K', Ghosuae came to be pronounced as Kosuae and it evolved into Koshy in Malayalam.
33. Korah	Refer to Kurien below. It has little to do with the name Korah appearing in the Psalms.
34. Koruthu	Same as Korah and Kurien

35. Kuriakose	**Meaning**: Kuria or Kuriye means 'The Lord' and Kuriakose means Lordly. **Origin**: Greek. Greek names ending in 'ose' (like Paulose, Phillipose, Kuriakose) are still commonly used by the Syrian Christians. Kuriye Elaisson said frequently in the Syrian Christian worship means 'Lord, have mercy'. Refer to Cyriac above.
36. Kurien	**Meaning**: The Lord. See Kuriakose. **Origin:** Greek. The Malayalam version of Kuriakose is Kurien. Omit the Greek suffix 'ose' and add the 'en'/'an', common for Malayalee male names.
37. Kurilose	**Meaning**: 'Lordly' derived from Greek – Kyrios/ Kuriye. (Lord). **Origin**: The Greek name Cyrilose, pronounced 'Koorilose' is used by the Syrian Christians only for their bishops or higher ecclesiastical hierarchies, as a title. Cyril is used sparingly for Syrian Christian men but the Syrian Christian counter-part Kuruvilla or Korula, is widely used.
38. Kuruvilla	**Meaning**: Lordly. Originates from Greek 'Kuriye'. See Kurilose. English version is Cyril.

39. Luke/ Lukose	**Meaning**: Light. **Origin**: Greek. New Testament author of the Gospel of Luke. The Greek name is Lukose, while in Latin it is Lucus or Lucas, and English Luke. Luke was a doctor of Greek background who travelled with the Apostle Paul and wrote Acts of the Apostles.
40. Mammen	**Meaning:** Same as Thomman. **Origin** – It is a form of Thomas which in Malayalam became Thomman, (add 'en/an'). Syrian Christians generally consider Mammen and Oommen to be derived from Thomman.

41. Mani	**Meaning and Origin** is unclear. In the West, the short form of Manuel is Manny and so it is argued that Mani is Manny and Manny is Manuel, which is Emmanuel. I do not agree that Mani is Manuel / Emmanuel. Mani (pronounced Maani) is mainly found in the Kottayam/Palai area of Travancore. If Mani was Manuel, at least some of them would have been christened as Manuel but Manuel is not a common name among the Syrian Christians. Note: Mani is also a Hindu short name (with Mani pronounced like Money). The Hindu Mani means jewel or a small round object. Can 'Maani' have originated from Mani? There is another Hindu name 'Maanikkam'. Is Maani the abbreviation of Maanikkam? Though, there are many Maanis, among Christians, one hardly comes across a Manikkam among them. In short, the origin of Mani, as a Christian name is not clear.
42. Mark/ Markose	**Origin**: The name Marcus is derived from the name of the Roman God Mars. Many first century Roman leaders were called Marcus including first century General Marcus Anthony (friend of Julius Caesar). New Testament, author of the Gospel of Mark or Markose in Greek and Malayalam. In English, it shortened to Mark. Markose is used by Syrian Christians.

43. Mathai/ Mathan/ Mathoo	**Meaning:** Gift of God. See Mathew. **Origin:** Mathai is the Syrian/Aramaic form of Mathew. Mathai was changed to Matthen in Malayalam. Mathoo is a colloquial version of Mathew. Note: The name is not derived from the 'Matthan' appearing in the genealogy of Jesus in Mathew 1 vs 15.
44. Mathew*/ Matthew	**Meaning**: Gift of God or Yahweh. **Origin**: The Greek name is Mathaios. Omit the 'os' to get Mathai (see above). Mathai was translated to Mathew in English. Matthew wrote the first book of the New Testament and was one of the twelve disciples of Jesus Christ. This English form is very popular among Syrian Christians.
45. Mathulla	**Meaning:** Gift of God. See Mathew. Math-ul-lah is like the Muslim name Habib-ul-la. Ul in Arabic appears to be 'of' and lah stands for Al lah/God. So Mathulla means gift of God, which has the same meaning as Mathew. This is not a common or frequently used name, except in a few families.

46. Ninan	**Meaning**: God is Gracious. Same as John/ Yohannan. **Origin**: This is a typical Syrian Christian name. The general opinion is that it is derived from Yohannan (English John). In the absence of any other rational explanation, I agree with the general opinion.
47. Oommen	See Thomas. **Origin**: This is derived from Thommen, which is the Malayalam version of Thoma, by adding 'en' or 'an' as suffix.
48. Ouseph/ Outha	See Joseph
49. Okkanden	See Alexander. It is a colloquial version of Alexander.
50. Pathappan	Malayalam form of Pathrose. See Pathrose.
51. Pathrose	**Meaning**: Rock. **Origin**: Greek. The name given by Jesus to the Apostle Simon was 'Cephas' which meant 'Rock' in Aramaic. The New Testament, written in Greek, translated the name to Pathrose or Pathar-ose which means 'rock' in Greek. Take away the 'ose' and you get Pathr or Pathar which in Arabic, Persian and even Hindi means rock or stone. The English name is Peter.

52. Paulose	**Meaning**: Small, Lesser, Little or Humble **Origin**: Paulus was a Roman family name in First Century BC. In the New Testament, it was the name of the early Christian leader, and Roman Jewish citizen, Paul (Hebrew name was Saul). Paul was the author of many books of the New Testament. He was later martyred and became Saint Paul. Paily, Piley (not Peeli), Pilo, are Malayalee short names for Paulose.
53. Peeli	See Philipose. Peeli/y is the Nazrani colloquial for Philiphose.
54. Peter*	**Meaning:** Rock **Origin:** See Pathrose above.
55. Philip/ Philipose	**Meaning**: Friend/Lover of horses. **Origin**: Greek Name derived from 'Philos' (friend) and 'Hippos' (horse). Philip II, was father of Alexander the Great of Macedon. New Testament name of one of the disciples of Jesus.

Syrian Christian Names

56. Pothen	Same as Philip. Generally accepted as the Malayalam counterpart of Philip. Remove the suffix of 'en'/'an' and we get Potha. The Syrian Christians rationalized it and said it is Phili-pochan (Philipose achan) shortened to Pochan by dropping the first part. Pochan evolved into Pothan. Note: It appears that 'Potha' is also a Dravidian name, Pothankodu is the name of a place in Kerala. Pothanoor is near Coimbatore.
57. Punnoose/ Punnen	**Meaning**; See Stephen. **Origin**: Greek. Remove the Greek suffix 'ose' from Punnoose and in Malayalam add an 'en'/'an' at the end to get Punnen. Stephanose in Greek was shortened to Phanos, then Panos and then to Punnoose. In the Kunnamkulan area, the name Panos is prevalent.
58. Samuel */ Shamuvel	**Meaning**: Name of God or God has heard. **Origin**: Old Testament. Hebrew name is Shemu'el. The El at the end means 'of God'. Shem means Name. Samuel is the last of the ruling Judges of the Old Testament. He was named by his mother, as God heard her prayers for a child. The English name is Samuel. In Malayalam, it is Shamuvel.
59. Skaria/ Karia	See Cherian.

60. Stephen*/ Stephanos	**Meaning**: Crown or 'that which surrounds'. **Origin**: New Testament deacon who was stoned to death as mentioned in the Acts of the Apostles. Greek name was Stephanose. Drop the 'ose' to derive the English name Stephen. Nazranis/Syrian Christians use the name Stephanos. See Punnoose.
61. Thomas/ Thoma/ Thommen	**Meaning**: Twin **Origin**: Greek form of the Aramaic name 'Ta'oma' which means twin. New Testament name of Christ's disciple, who was often referred to as 'doubting' Thomas. It is the most frequently occurring name for Syrian Christians because St Thomas was considered the founder of Christianity in Kerala and the Syrian Christians were known as Thoma Christians or St Thomas Christians, at one time.
62. Timothy	**Meaning**: To Honour God or Honouring God **Origin**: Greek name is Timotheous. In Greek, Theos means God and Timao means 'To Honour'. New Testament, name of Paul's companion on his missionary journeys and two epistles named after him. Not a common Syrian Christian Name. Timotheos is a title adopted by Syrian Christian (Orthodox and Mar Thoma) Bishops.

63. Titus	**Meaning**: unknown. **Origin**: A Roman name in the First Century. The Greek version is also Titus but pronounced as Teethoose. The English name is Titus, and the preferred name by Syrian Christians. Its Malayalam version is Datose. Titus is used by the Bishops as a surname or title.
64. Ulahannan	See John.
65. Uthup	See Joseph.

66. Varghese/ Verghese	**Meaning**: Farmer, worker of earth. Also see George. **Origin**: This name is derived from Greek word Georgeose. The Malayalam name is Gee Varghese. The letter 'G' has two sounds; one like the letter 'j' as in 'germ' and the other as in 'God'. In the name Georgeose or Giorgiose the 'g' has the sound as in God. Georgeose would sound as Gee Orgheose. In Malayalam, when two vowels are joined together, a 'v' sound is used to conjoin them; so 'Gee Orgheose' became Gee Varghese. (See Guidelines Chapter). Over time, the Gee was omitted in GeeVarghese and became Varghese, which is the most common Syrian Christian male name, along with Thomas. Varghese was further shortened to 'Varghe'. As stated earlier, the Dravidians didn't have a 'ga' sound. 'Ga' became 'ka' and 'gi' became 'ki'. Varghe became Varki. Varghese also formed 'Vareed' in Thrissur /Kunnamkulam area.

67. Xavier	**Meaning**: Saviour. This is not a Nazrani/Syrian Christian name but Xavier is prevalent among the Catholics of Kerala primarily. **Origin**: This was the surname of the Jesuit priest Saint Francis Xavier in the 16th Century who was born in a village of this name in Spain. He was a missionary to Goa, India (which was under Portuguese rule). The name is used in his honor among the Catholics.
68. Yohannan	See John.
69. Zachariah.	**Meaning**: Yahweh/God remembers. **Origin**: Old Testament minor prophet, who wrote the Book of Zachariah. Also, New Testament, name of the priest and father of John the Baptist. Origin is a Hebrew name. This English name is more prevalent than its Malayalam Syrian Christian counterpart Skaria or Karia. Syrian Christians prefer the name Cheria/Cherian which means Zachariah.

Syrian Christian Female Names

If Syrian Christians have only a very limited number of male or masculine names, they have a much smaller number of feminine names. Given below are the common Nazrani feminine names.

NAME	MEANING AND ORIGIN.
1. Aachy	**Meaning**: Name of flower/Lily. **Origin**: To make it an acceptable Christian name, it has been claimed to originate from Susan, short for Susana. Susana is a chapter in the Book of Daniel in the Catholic Bible. The Hebrew name is Shoshana, which is a flower like Lily. Shoshana was shortened to Shosha. To show how is Aachy the same as Susan/Shoshana, you need to go by phonetics. Shosha, Shesha, Checha, Chachi, Aachy, Acha. This is a popular name for Syrian Christian women and women in Tamil Nadu, even today. Syrian Christians originally spoke Tamil or a variation of that language, for centuries and Achy was a name popular with them also.
2. Acca	**Meaning**: In Tamil means elder sister. **Origin**: The Nazrani Christians used to have Acca as a name like Aachy, but mainly as a pet name. Since they have to have a Biblical name, it was

		claimed that Acca (Akka) was a short form of Rebecca. It is also widely used among Tamilian non-Christians. Claiming Acca as a short form of Rebecca is only an attempt to link it to the Bible. The name is used as a mark of respect. Usage of Acca is common in Kerala also even now.
3.	Acha/ Achamma	**Meaning/Origin –** see Aachy above. Achamma is derived by adding amma to Acha. It is a very popular name for Nazrani ladies.
4.	Anna	**Meaning**: Grace, Graceful **Origin**: Old Testament, Hebrew name is Hannah. She is the mother, blessed with a son Samuel, by the Temple priest in the Old Testament. (Samuel later anoints David as King of the Jews). In English, the H is lost and it becomes Anna. This Nazrani name is quite popular with various prefixes and suffixes like Koch-Anna, Kunju Anna, Annamma, Annakutty in Malayalam and English variations like Ann, Anne, Annie, Anita are also popular with Syrian Christians.
5.	Chinna	**Meaning**: In Tamil it means small, young or junior. **Origin**: For Nazranis, it is widely used especially among the Syrian Christians of Central Travancore. There has been a faint-hearted attempt in some quarters to claim that 'Chinna' was another form of Anna. That does not make sense, since Chinnan, Chinnakutty, Chinnachen are used for men. Chinnan cannot be

	Annan,and Chinnachan cannot be considered to be Annachan! Chinna is widely used as a personal name among Tamilians and among Malayalees, Christian and non-Christians.
6. Dinah	**Meaning**: Judged. **Origin**: Hebrew, Old Testament. Only daughter of Jacob from his wife Leah.
7. Eli/ Ailey Eliamma	**Origin/Meaning**- See Elizabeth. The E is pronounced like 'A' in Abraham, or area. Eli is short for Elizabeth.
8. Elizabeth*	**Meaning**: Consecrated by God. **Origin**: Old Testament Hebrew form is Elisheva. New Testament name of the mother of John the Baptist. Variations among Syrian Christians exist like Aeley, Elia, Elacha. English variations like Lisa, Lizzy, Ella are also popular with Syrian Christians.
9. Maria/ Mariam/ Mary	**Meaning**: Unclear. Most likely means 'love'. Some give the meaning as 'bitter' but this does not appear accurate. People do not give unpleasant names to their children and Miriam was a popular name. It is the most commonly appearing name for women in the New Testament. **Origin**: Most likely it is of Egyptian origin derived from the word Mry for 'love'. Miriyam is

	the Old Testament Hebrew name of the sister of Moses. In the Greek New Testament, Miriyam/ Mariam was the name of the mother of Jesus. The English shortened the name to Mary. The misconception about 'bitter' arose because the word "MARA' in the Bible meant 'bitter'. Mara is akin to Marine or Maritime from the word Mars, which meant the 'sea', and its water is salty or bitter.
10. Rachel*/ Rahel	**Meaning**: Wikipedia gives the meaning as 'ewe' of Lamb. This seems reasonable, as Rachel (in the Old Testament) is the daughter of Laban, who owned a lot of flock, so naming his daughter 'ewe' seems possible. **Origin**: Old Testament, Hebrew Rachel is the wife of Jacob, and mother of Joseph (who was transported to Egypt). Rachel in English, is derived from the Jewish name 'Raqel' or Raqhel, or Rachel with the 'ch' pronounced as in 'character' or 'chord'. In English, the 'ch' in Rachel is pronounced like the 'ch' in church. In Malayalam, Raqel became Rahel.
11. Rapukka	See Rebecca. In Tamil and Malayalam, 'b' is substituted by 'p' and the Jewish Rabekka became Rapukka for the Syrian Christians. (Also see Acca/Akka above)

12. Rebecca*	**Meaning**: To tie firmly **Origin**- Old Testament, wife of Isaac, and mother of Esau and Jacob. Other forms, Becky, Becca, Reba. The original Nazrani name is Rapukka. Rebecca is the English name.
13. Sarah	**Meaning**: Princess **Origin**: Old Testament wife of Abraham. Her original name was Sarai but God changed it to Sarah in Genesis. Greek name is Sarra.
14. Shosha	See Aachy
15. Susan/ Susy	See Aachy
16. Thanda	Colloquial for Sarah. See Sarah.
17. Thoya	Colloquial for Shosha
18. Theyya	Colloquial for Thressia (Theresa). Theresa is a European name, not a Nazrani name.

Titles used as Surnames by Nazranis

There are three titles used as surnames by Syrian Christians or Nazranis. They are Muthalaly, Panikkar and Tharakan.

Background

The area called the State of Travancore (Southern Kerala), was ruled by Rajas and chieftains. The Syrian Christians formed a sizable portion of the population of this area. They were mainly farmers and traders. Some of them were good at Martial arts and proved their military prowess by helping the local army. In recognition of all their assistance, the various Rajas/ chieftains honoured them with titles. This practice continued even after the formation of the princely States of Kochy and Travancore. The most mentionable titles given were Muthalaly, Panikkar and Tharakan.

Muthalaly

Muthalaly is not a Biblical name. The word 'Muthal' in Malayalam means wealth and Muthalaly means one who has plenty of wealth. At the time when they received the title, they might have been wealthy traders/ business men.

In Malayalam, this word is used in contrast with' Thozhilaly'. Thozhil means work and a Thozhilaly is a labourer. Most of these wealthy Muthalalies or their Muthalali ancestors were from Central Travancore. The successive generations used this title as a last name, or as a name only.

Syrian Christian Names

Panikkar

Panikkars are from the Nair community. Panikkar denoted one who is well versed in martial arts. This title was bestowed on Nazranis, whose military prowess helped the local chieftain. These Panikkars were mainly from a few Nazrani families in and around Kundara, near Kollam.

Today one might come across Yohannan Panikkar, Mathai Panikkar etc. as later generations used the title as a surname.

Tharakan

Thara in Malayalam means 'floor' or 'land'. The word Tharawad arose from the word Thara or family land. Many family names have 'thara' as suffix to show or denote land or the place to stay. Example: Kaniyan thara meaning Kaniyan's land. Tharakan is a person who has land. In the old days, land in Kerala and in India was the most valuable and visible asset. Any person who had a lot of land was a very important person and deserved honour. Hence the Title 'Tharakan' was given to him by the local rulers. This is equivalent to the North Indian title of Zamindar, where Zamin means Land.

Tharakan was the Malayalee Zamindar, this title was bestowed on big Nazrani land holders and like other titles, was inherited by successive generations.

Ordained Names of Bishops

When Syrian Christian Priests (Orthodox/ Mar thoma) are ordained as Bishops, they take a new name like the Popes do, when they are elevated to the papal throne. Most of the surnames of the Bishops are Greek names like Basseleose / Basiliose (Basil), Koorilose (Cyril), Dionysius(Dione) Philexinose (Felix) and are prefixed by the word "Mar' meaning Saint or Saintly. Example Yakub Mar Timotheose. These are very seldom used as personal names by Syrian Christians.   The Bishops are given the names of Church leaders of the early Church, the ones who were made Saints or had made special theological contributions to the early church.

The Syrian Christian 'Pet' names

The Syrian Christians of Kerala had their children, boys and girls baptised with Christian names but at home, the children were given 'pet' names by which the parents and close relatives addressed them.

In the ancient days, the common pet name for boys and girls was 'Kunju' meaning 'baby' or 'junior' as a term of endearment. Examples were Kochu kunju, Kunju kutty for boys and Kunj-amma or Kunju-mol for girls. It was common to see a large family where all the boys and girls were called some variation of Kunju. This tradition continued for centuries.

From around 1870 to the turn of the century, two names became very popular, for boys. They are Baby and Thamby. They found places among almost half the central Travancore Christians, sometimes both in the same family, usually Baby preceding Thamby. Baby, is derived from English. It is the English equivalent of Malayalam Kunju. When Syrian Christians started to speak English, some parents started naming their sons Baby instead of Kunju. It almost became what we might call 'viral'. Soon girls also started getting the moniker Baby. If Baby is from English, Thamby is from Tamil and means little or younger brother.

Revolutionary Change.

By the mid-20th century, Syrian Christians started a change in the lack luster system of pet names for their children. New names without much meaning, like the names of new products, appeared on the scene. One can see them from reading the Obituary reports in the Malayala Manorama newspaper, where they note the names of the children of the departed ones. Most of the new names are gender neutral, community, or nationality neutral and can apply to boys or girls.

Some examples are given below:

Abi, Beebi, Ceebi, Deebi Feebi, Geebi.

Cinto, Dinto, Linto,Minto, Pinto.

 Bijo, Cijo, Jijo, Shijo, Shany, Sheeny, Shiny, Shony

This does not mean that parents have forgotten their Syrian Christian roots. Even though the children are given trendy names of the current, they are baptized formally with a Christian Name.

About the Author

Wing Commander Kurien Verghese graduated from Madras Christian College, and has a MA, LLB from Bombay University. He is a Retired Officer of the Indian Air Force from the Legal Branch where he was Command Judge Advocate.

Kurien Verghese, among other things, has an interest in linguistics and word origins. He has spent considerable time researching Syrian Christian Names. He enjoys reading, playing badminton and cards in his retired years.

Kurien Verghese belongs to the Kozhimannil family of Thiruvalla, Kerala. He recently celebrated his 91st birthday and resides with his wife in Koramangala, Bangalore.

Published Nov 2017